Let's Read About Pets

Rabbits

by JoAnn Early Macken

Reading consultant: Susan Nations, M.Ed., author/literacy coach/consultant

WEEKLY WR READER®
EARLY LEARNING LIBRARY

Please visit our web site at: www.earlyliteracy.cc
For a free color catalog describing Weekly Reader® Early Learning Library's
list of high-quality books, call 1-877-445-5824 (USA) or 1-800-387-3178 (Canada).
Weekly Reader® Early Learning Library's fax: (414) 336-0164.

Library of Congress Cataloging-in-Publication Data

Macken, JoAnn Early, 1953-
    Rabbits / by JoAnn Early Macken.
        p. cm. — (Let's read about pets)
    Summary: Simple text and pictures briefly describe the physical characteristics
and behavior of rabbits and how to care for them as pets.
    Includes bibliographical references and index.
    ISBN 0-8368-3802-5 (lib. bdg.)
    ISBN 0-8368-3849-1 (softcover)
    1. Rabbits—Juvenile literature. [1. Rabbits as pets. 2. Pets.] I. Title.
SF453.2.M23   2003
636.9'322—dc21   2003045015

First published in 2004 by
Weekly Reader® Early Learning Library
330 West Olive Street, Suite 100
Milwaukee, WI 53212 USA

Editorial: JoAnn Early Macken
Art direction: Tammy Gruenewald
Page layout: Katherine A. Goedheer

Printed in the United States of America

1 2 3 4 5 6 7 8 9 07 06 05 04 03

Note to Educators and Parents

Reading is such an exciting adventure for young children! They are beginning to integrate their oral language skills with written language. To encourage children along the path to early literacy, books must be colorful, engaging, and interesting; they should invite the young reader to explore both the print and the pictures.

Let's Read About Pets is a new series designed to help children learn about the joys and responsibilities of keeping a pet. In each book, young readers will learn interesting facts about the featured animal and how to care for it.

Each book is specially designed to support the young reader in the reading process. The familiar topics are appealing to young children and invite them to read — and re-read — again and again. The full-color photographs and enhanced text further support the student during the reading process.

In addition to serving as wonderful picture books in schools, libraries, homes, and other places where children learn to love reading, these books are specifically intended to be read within an instructional guided reading group. This small group setting allows beginning readers to work with a fluent adult model as they make meaning from the text. After children develop fluency with the text and content, the book can be read independently. Children and adults alike will find these books supportive, engaging, and fun!

— Susan Nations, M.Ed., author, literacy coach,
and consultant in literacy development

Newborn rabbits have no fur. They cannot see, hear, or hop. In two months, they are old enough to be pets.

5

Rabbits may have short fur or long fur. Rabbits with long fur must be brushed more often.

A rabbit's fur may be brown, black, white, or other colors. It may have spots or patterns.

To hear better, rabbits can move their ears. Some rabbits have ears that droop. These rabbits are called "lops."

A rabbit uses its **whiskers** to find its way in the dark. It can fit into a space as wide as its whiskers.

whiskers

Rabbits eat food in pellets. They also need fresh water and hay. They like carrots, parsley, and other vegetables.

A rabbit can live in a cage or a hutch. It can go outside in good weather.

A rabbit might thump its feet if it is scared. It might sit up to see or smell something.

Rabbits can roll balls. They can hop in and out of things. Give your rabbit a toy and watch it play!

Glossary

hay — dried grass or other plants fed to animals

hutch — a pen or cage for an animal

pellets — small pieces of food

thump — to pound or knock

For More Information

Fiction Books

Fleming, Candace. *Muncha! Muncha! Muncha!*
   New York: Atheneum Books for Young Readers, 2002.
McCarty, Peter. *Little Bunny on the Move.*
   New York: Henry Holt, 1999.

Nonfiction Books

Gibbons, Gail. *Rabbits, Rabbits, & More Rabbits!*
   New York: Holiday House, 2000.
Klingel, Cynthia Fitterer and Noyed, Robert B. *Rabbits.*
   Chanhassen, Minn.: Child's World, 2001.

Web Sites
House Rabbit Society's Kids' Page
www.rabbit.org/kids/
Links to pictures, stories, and fun facts about rabbits

Index

About the Author

JoAnn Early Macken is the author of two rhyming picture books, *Sing-Along Song* and *Cats on Judy*, and three other series of nonfiction books. She teaches children to write poetry, and her poems have appeared in several children's magazines. A graduate of the M.F.A. in Writing for Children and Young Adults program at Vermont College, she lives in Wisconsin with her husband and their two sons.